The Integrated Homeschool

Book 1: Building the Foundation

A Guide to Learning with Heart, Mind, and Purpose

By D.R. Pack

An educator-informed approach to homeschooling

Copyright & Publication Information

Print ISBN: 978-1-7644066-4-2
First edition
Published by D.R. Pack Publishing. Printed globally.

How to Use This Book

Welcome to the first book in The Integrated Homeschool series.

This book is designed as your architectural blueprint --- the foundational vision and structural framework for building a homeschool that honours your child's unique strengths while maintaining educational rigour.

What This Book Is

This is Book 1 of a possible four-part series. It provides:

- **The Philosophy**: Why learning organised around the Element and Learning Expeditions creates deeper, more meaningful education
- **The Framework**: How to observe your child, recognise patterns, and design learning experiences that fit
- **The Vision**: A clear picture of what integrated, inquiry-based homeschooling looks like in practice

What This Book Is Not

This is not a day-by-day curriculum guide. It doesn't cover specialised strategies for neurodivergent learners or secondary education planning. Instead, it lays the groundwork that makes all those practical applications possible.

How to Read This Book

If you're brand new to homeschooling:
Read straight through from Introduction to Chapter 7, then explore the Appendix templates as you're ready to try them.

If you're already homeschooling but feel stuck:
Start with Part I (Chapters 1-4) to reconnect with your child's natural learning patterns, then jump to Part II (Chapters 5-6) to redesign your approach.

If you're confident in your philosophy but need structure:
Begin with Chapter 5 (What Is a Learning Expedition?) and use the Appendix templates immediately.

Working With the Series

- **Book 1** (this book): The vision and framework
- **Proposed Book 2**: Daily rhythms, scheduling, and practical implementation
- **Proposed Book 3**: Adaptations for neurodivergent learners and learning differences
- **Proposed Book 4**: Secondary education, portfolio building, and post-school pathways

Each book will build on this foundation, but Book 1 is essential reading for everyone.

A Note on Templates

The Appendix contains practical tools referenced throughout the book. Don't feel pressured to use every template. Choose what serves you, adapt freely, and return to tools as your confidence grows.

The Tools & Templates are free to download at:

https://dennispack.gumroad.com/l/theintegratedhomeschool

Access is optional and not required to use this book.

About Diverse Learners

Throughout this book, you'll notice brief "call-outs" in highlighted boxes addressing how concepts apply to diverse learners --- including neurodivergent children, anxious learners, and twice-exceptional students. A future book may expand these ideas comprehensively, but these call-outs ensure the framework works for all children from the start.

Introduction: How We Ended Up Here

I didn't set out to homeschool.

I assumed school would work the way it was supposed to. If we chose carefully, stayed involved, and trusted the process, things would fall into place. For a while, they did --- or at least it seemed that way.

Then the small things started adding up.

Learning slowly became something to get through instead of something to explore. Curiosity narrowed. Confidence wavered. I noticed how much effort went into meeting expectations, and how little went into understanding why the work mattered in the first place.

Nothing was obviously "wrong."

That was the problem.

There were no dramatic failures, just a quiet sense that something essential was being missed. Outside of school, my child was capable, persistent, and curious. Inside the system, those same qualities seemed irrelevant --- or inconvenient.

The idea of homeschooling arrived gradually, and with it came doubt. Was I qualified? Would there be gaps? Was I being unrealistic to think I could offer something better?

What surprised me was the realisation that I already knew how my child learnt best. I adjusted explanations, followed interests, and encouraged persistence without calling it education. I had been teaching all along --- I just hadn't trusted that it counted.

Homeschooling didn't begin with confidence.

It began with responsibility.

Clarifying the Author's Voice

The story you just read is not my own.

It is a composite --- drawn from years of conversations with parents who arrived at homeschooling thoughtfully, reluctantly, and often with a great deal of self-doubt. While the details differ, the pattern is remarkably consistent.

This book is written from a different vantage point.

I write as an educator --- someone who has spent years studying how people learn, watching what engages students deeply, and observing what happens when education is built around human development rather than institutional convenience. My goal is not to romanticise homeschooling, nor to position parents as replacement teachers.

My goal is to help the homeschooling community do what schools often struggle to do well: create learning that is meaningful, rigorous, and responsive to the individual child.

Foundations of This Handbook

The framework in this book is grounded in three complementary influences.

From **Sir Ken Robinson**, I draw the conviction that education should help learners discover their strengths and purpose --- not force them into narrow definitions of success. His work clarifies why standardisation so often suppresses talent rather than develops it.

From **Eddie Woo**, I take the example of what excellent teaching actually looks like: depth over speed, clarity over coverage, and respect for the learner's capacity to think. His classroom practice demonstrates that rigour and humanity are not opposing forces.

And from the **Expeditionary Learning (EL) school model**, I borrow structure. EL schools show how learning can be organised around extended enquiries, authentic work, and character development --- providing coherence without sacrificing curiosity.

This handbook translates and integrates those ideas into a homeschool context.

It is not a curriculum, but a framework. Not a set of rules, but a way of making decisions. It is written to support parents who want to take education seriously without replicating the very systems they stepped away from.

What follows is an invitation to think differently about learning --- and to do so with intention, confidence, and care.

The Three Pillars: Heart, Mind, and Adventure

This book is grounded in three complementary ideas: the importance of discovering a child's unique strengths, following curiosity rather than completion, and learning through meaningful, real-world work. Together, they form the foundation for the approach that follows.

The Heart: Sir Ken Robinson's Philosophy

- Nurturing "The Element" --- the meeting point of aptitude and passion
- Valuing unique spark and diverse intelligence
- The gardener metaphor: creating conditions for growth
- Permission to be wrong and learn through exploration

The Mind: Eddie Woo's Methods

- Maths as a "sense" --- pattern recognition across all learning
- Slowing down to ask "Why?"
- Lighting a fire, not filling a pail
- Mathematics as social power and tool for understanding

The Adventure: Expeditionary Learning

- Learning Expeditions and real-world problems
- The primacy of self-discovery
- High-quality products for real audiences
- Service and compassion built into the process

Together, these three pillars provide a compass to navigate the open seas of learning, leading to a purposeful and inspired journey.

This book is grounded in three complementary ideas: the importance of discovering a child's unique strengths, following curiosity rather than completion, and learning through meaningful, real-world work. Together, they form the foundation for the approach that follows.

PART I:

Understanding Your Child

Chapter 1: The Element --- When Learning Finally Feels Like It Fits

Most parents can recognise the moment.

Your child is absorbed in something --- building, drawing, explaining, experimenting, rehearsing, fixing. You call their name and they don't hear you. Time seems to disappear. When they finally look up, they're energised rather than exhausted.

This is not an accident.

And it's not just enjoyment.

Sir Ken Robinson called this experience **the Element**.

The Element is the meeting point between natural aptitude and personal passion --- the place where the things a child is naturally good at and the things they deeply care about come together. It isn't just about ability, and it isn't just about interest. It's about alignment.

When children are in their Element, learning stops feeling forced. Effort feels worthwhile. They feel most like themselves. Not because the work is easy, but because it is meaningful.

Robinson emphasised that the Element is not merely a skill set --- it is connected to a person's identity, sense of purpose, and wellbeing. In this state, learners are often capable of far more than anyone expects, including themselves. They stretch, persist, and improve not because they're chasing approval, but because they are internally motivated.

Parents sometimes describe this as seeing "the real version" of their child.

Being "In the Zone": Why the Element Feels Different

A defining feature of the Element is what many people call being in the zone. Psychologists refer to it as a state of flow --- when a person is so deeply engaged in a process that time passes almost unnoticed and ideas seem to emerge naturally.

In this state, a child's skills are well matched to the challenge in front of them. The work is demanding, but not overwhelming. Because of that balance, being in the Element doesn't drain energy --- it generates it.

This is why children can spend hours on something they love and emerge alert, satisfied, and eager to continue, while thirty minutes of disconnected work can leave them exhausted or resistant.

The Element is not about escaping difficulty.

It's about finding the kind of difficulty that fits.

Why the Element Is So Rare in Traditional Education

Traditional schooling often operates on what Robinson called a "swarm" model --- large numbers of students moving through the same content in the same way, at the same time. In that environment, individuality becomes a complication rather than a strength.

The Element quietly resists this logic.

It recognises that human intelligence is not uniform, but diverse, dynamic, and deeply distinctive. Each child brings a different combination of abilities, interests, rhythms, and ways of making sense of the world. When education honours that reality, learning becomes personal rather than performative.

This is why discovering the Element often feels like a revelation. It isn't that something new has been added to the child --- it's that something essential has finally been recognised.

A Helpful Way to Think About the Element

Think of the Element as a key finding its lock.

Natural aptitude is the shape of the key.
Personal passion is the hand that turns it.

You can have one without the other, but nothing opens until they meet.
When they do, a door swings open --- to confidence, purpose, and
growth that feels authentic rather than imposed.

For homeschooling families, this understanding changes everything.

It shifts the focus from "covering material" to cultivating alignment.
From asking, *Are we keeping up?* to asking, *Is my child becoming
more themselves through learning?*

In the next section, we'll explore why this alignment matters not just
now, but for a child's entire life as a learner --- and how homeschooling
uniquely positions families to help children find it.

Pause and Reflect: Noticing the Element

Before reading on, take a moment to think about your child --- not as a
student, but as a person.

You're not trying to identify their Element yet. You're simply paying
attention.

Consider these questions:

- When does your child seem most absorbed in what they're
  doing?
- What activities make time disappear for them?
- When do they persist through difficulty without being pushed?
- What kinds of challenges energise them rather than frustrate
  them?
- When have you thought, *This feels like the real version of my
  child*?

You may notice patterns. You may notice contradictions. You may
notice nothing clear at all --- and that's completely normal.

Element discovery is not a moment; it's a process. Many children reveal it gradually, and often in unexpected ways. Your role right now is not to define or label, but to observe with curiosity rather than judgement.

As you continue through this chapter, keep your child in mind. The examples and ideas that follow are not meant to narrow your thinking, but to help you recognise what may already be unfolding.

Case Study: Finding the Element Without Looking for It

When Maya's parents began homeschooling, they were primarily trying to reduce stress.

Maya was ten years old and capable, but school had become a daily struggle. She completed assignments, but reluctantly. Reading felt laborious. Maths felt disconnected. Teachers described her as polite, creative, and "easily distracted."

At home, however, a different picture emerged.

Maya spent hours drawing. Not casually --- intentionally. She filled notebooks with characters, scenes, symbols, and patterns. She revised constantly, erasing and redrawing details most adults wouldn't notice. When frustrated, she didn't quit. She adjusted.

At first, her parents treated this as something separate from learning --- something to be done after schoolwork was finished. But over time, they noticed something important: drawing was the only activity where Maya consistently entered what could only be described as deep focus.

Time disappeared. Resistance vanished.

Instead of trying to channel this interest into formal art instruction immediately, her parents did something quieter. They paid attention.

They noticed that Maya:

- Asked thoughtful questions about visual storytelling
- Analysed illustrations in books more carefully than the text
- Remembered historical details better when they were tied to images
- Persisted longer when tasks involved design or visual problem-solving

Gradually, they began to adapt learning around these observations.

Reading shifted towards graphic novels, illustrated biographies, and art history texts. Writing emerged through character backstories and visual narratives. History became a study of symbols, architecture, and design across cultures. Even maths found its way in through scaling, proportion, and perspective.

What mattered most was not that Maya "became an artist."

What mattered was that learning finally fit.

Her Element was not simply drawing. It was making meaning visually. The aptitude had always been there. The passion created the doorway. When they met, engagement followed.

Two years later, Maya's academic skills had strengthened significantly --- but more importantly, her relationship with learning had changed. She no longer asked, "Do I have to?" She asked, "Can I show you?"

Why This Case Matters

Maya's story is not remarkable because it is rare. It is remarkable because it is common.

Element discovery rarely arrives as a lightning bolt. It emerges through careful observation, permission to linger, and adults willing to treat curiosity as a signal rather than a distraction.

For homeschooling families, this is powerful reassurance: you don't need to manufacture motivation. You need to notice where it already exists --- and make room for it to grow.

> **Note for Diverse Learners:**
> For children with ADHD, autism, or anxiety, the Element often appears in hyperfocus states or special interests. What looks like "obsession" to others may actually be the clearest signal of where aptitude and passion align. Trust these signals --- they're often more reliable than standardised assessments.

Chapter 2: The Four-Part Element Discovery Process

Finding a child's Element is not a personality test, a single conversation, or a one-time insight. It's a process --- one that unfolds over time through attention, opportunity, and reflection.

The good news is that homeschooling naturally creates the conditions for this work. You have proximity. You see how your child learns when no one is grading them. You witness what happens when pressure is removed.

This chapter offers a four-part process for Element discovery. It isn't linear, and it isn't rigid. Families often cycle through these steps multiple times as children grow and change. The purpose is not to "pin down" a child's future, but to recognise patterns that point towards meaningful learning now.

Step 1: Observe Without Agenda

The first and most important step is also the hardest --- especially for conscientious parents.

Observe without trying to direct, fix, or interpret too quickly.

This means resisting the urge to turn every interest into a lesson, every strength into a plan, and every moment into a measurement.

Element discovery begins with noticing, not steering.

What to Watch For

When observing your child, pay particular attention to:

- **Flow states**: When do they become so absorbed that time seems to disappear?
- **Voluntary practice**: What do they return to without reminders or rewards?
- **Natural questions**: What do they wonder about repeatedly or independently?

These signals often show up quietly and inconsistently at first. They are easy to miss if you're focused primarily on output.

The "Boredom Test"

One surprisingly revealing tool is boredom.

When nothing is required --- no assignments, no screens, no plans --- what does your child gravitate towards?

Boredom strips away performance and compliance. What remains often points towards genuine interest. It may not look impressive or academic, but it is usually honest.

Keeping an Observation Journal

Rather than trying to remember everything, write it down.

A simple observation journal --- just a few notes per week --- is enough. Record what your child chose to do, how long they stayed with it, and how they responded to challenge or interruption.

There is no analysis required at this stage. The goal is accumulation, not conclusion. A template is provided in the Appendix to help structure this process without overcomplicating it.

Step 2: Create a Low-Stakes Exploration Buffet

Observation alone isn't enough. Children also need exposure.

Many Elements remain undiscovered simply because a child has never encountered the field or problem space where their aptitude and passion align.

Think of this step as offering a buffet, not assigning a meal.

Exposing Children to Diverse Experiences

Exploration does not require elaborate planning. Small, varied experiences are often more effective than deep dives too early.

This might include:

- Short-term projects
- Guest workshops or classes
- Field trips and virtual tours
- Books, documentaries, and demonstrations
- Casual hands-on experiences at home

The key is low commitment. Children should feel free to sample without the pressure to excel or continue.

The Importance of Productive Failure

Exploration includes things that don't work --- and that's not a problem.

Trying something and deciding it's not a good fit is valuable information. It sharpens self-awareness and builds discernment. When failure is treated as data rather than disappointment, children learn how to evaluate experiences honestly.

Homeschooling allows this kind of failure without long-term consequences. Use that freedom.

Community Resources Matter

You don't need to do this alone.

Libraries, maker spaces, sports clubs, arts organisations, mentors, and online communities offer low-barrier entry points into many fields. Often, a single conversation with someone who loves what they do is enough to spark meaningful curiosity.

Step 3: Listen to Their Questions

As exploration continues, something subtle begins to shift. Children move from trying things to wondering about things.

This is where listening becomes more important than planning.

From "What Do You Want to Be?" to "What Fascinates You?"

Future-focused questions often shut children down. They imply permanence before clarity exists.

Instead, listen for questions like:

- Why does this work the way it does?
- What would happen if...?
- How could this be better?
- Who decided this?

These questions point towards underlying interests --- not outcomes, but problems and patterns that capture attention.

Eddie Woo's Principle: Follow Curiosity, Not Completion

One of Eddie Woo's most powerful teaching principles is prioritising understanding over finishing. Completion is external. Curiosity is internal.

When children ask questions, resist the urge to rush them towards answers. Sit with the question. Encourage exploration. Let understanding unfold unevenly.

Depth matters more than speed.

Deep vs. Superficial Interest

Not every interest leads to the Element.

Superficial interests fade when novelty wears off. Deep interests grow more complex over time. They generate better questions, longer engagement, and a willingness to struggle.

Your role is not to judge, but to notice which interests deepen when given space.

Step 4: Identify the Through-Line

Over time, patterns begin to emerge.

This is where Element discovery becomes clearer --- not because you've found a label, but because you've identified a through-line.

Pattern Recognition Across Interests

A child's interests may look unrelated on the surface: storytelling, history, debate, and role-playing games. But the underlying through-line might be *making sense of human motivation*.

Another child may cycle through coding, puzzles, building, and strategy games. The through-line may be *systems thinking*.

Look beneath the activity to the way your child engages with it.

The Aptitude + Passion Intersection

The Element lives at the intersection of:

- What your child does with increasing skill
- What your child returns to with increasing interest

When those two curves rise together, pay attention.

This is not a declaration of destiny. It is a signal of alignment.

Mapping the Element

To support this step, the Appendix includes a worksheet that helps you map observations, interests, questions, and patterns in one place. A sample is included on the next page. Many parents find that simply laying everything out visually brings clarity they didn't expect.

Remember: the Element is not something you assign. It's something you recognise.

A Reassuring Note

Some children reveal their Element early. Others take time. Many move through several Elements across childhood and adolescence.

That is not failure --- it is development.

The purpose of this process is not to narrow your child's future, but to help them experience learning that feels authentic, engaging, and humane right now.

- **Note for Diverse Learners:**
Children with learning differences may show aptitude in non-traditional ways. A child with dyslexia might demonstrate exceptional spatial reasoning. A child with ADHD might excel at divergent thinking. The Element Discovery Process works particularly well for theselearners because it prioritises observation over standardised measurement.

Sample worksheet from the downloadable Appendix: Tools & Templates

Tool 1.2: Element Mapping Worksheet

Purpose: To look for through-lines across multiple observations.

When to use: After 4-6 weeks of observation journaling.

How to use:

- Review your observation journal entries
- Look for patterns across different activities
- Focus on *how* your child engages, not just *what* they do
- Hold conclusions lightly—this is a working hypothesis, not a diagnosis

Template:

ELEMENT MAPPING WORKSHEET

Child's name: ___________________   Age: ______   Date: ___________

SECTION 1: APTITUDES I NOTICE

What does my child seem naturally good at?
(Examples: spatial reasoning, pattern recognition, narrative thinking, social connection, physical coordination, musical sense, systems thinking)

1. ____
2. ____
3. ____

Evidence for each:

____

____

SECTION 2: INTERESTS AND FASCINATIONS

What topics, activities, or problems capture their attention repeatedly?

1. ____
2. ____
3. ____

What do these interests have in common? ___________________________________

____

Chapter 3: What If I Can't Find It Yet?

At some point, almost every homeschooling parent asks a version of the same question:

What if I'm doing all of this --- and I still can't see my child's Element?

This question usually comes from care, not doubt. It comes from parents who are observing thoughtfully, offering opportunities, listening carefully --- and still feel unsure. The silence can feel loud.

This chapter exists to say something clearly and early:

Not finding the Element yet does not mean you're failing --- or that your child is missing something essential.

In fact, uncertainty is often a sign that development is still unfolding exactly as it should.

The Element Is Not a One-Time Discovery

One of the most common misunderstandings about the Element is the belief that it is a single, defining revelation --- something that appears suddenly and then remains fixed.

That is rarely how it works.

The Element is not a destination. It is a relationship between aptitude, passion, and opportunity --- and relationships evolve. What fits a child at seven may feel constricting at fourteen. What feels impractical at ten may become powerful later with maturity and context.

In education, we often confuse clarity with certainty. But healthy learning allows for ambiguity.

For many children, the Element becomes visible only in retrospect. Parents often recognise patterns years later and think, *Of course --- that was there all along*. At the time, it simply looked like curiosity, restlessness, or experimentation.

Your role is not to force clarity prematurely. It is to protect the conditions that allow clarity to emerge.

Multiple Elements and Shifting Passions

Some children don't have one Element --- they have several.

They may move between domains, draw energy from different kinds of work, or combine interests in unexpected ways. This does not indicate a lack of focus. It often signals cognitive flexibility, breadth of curiosity, or integrative thinking.

A child might:

- Love storytelling and logical puzzles
- Move between artistic expression and analytical reasoning
- Cycle through interests seasonally or developmentally

Rather than asking, *Which one is real?* it can be more useful to ask, *What do these interests have in common?*

The through-line may not be a subject at all. It may be:

- Making sense of complexity
- Explaining ideas to others
- Designing systems
- Exploring human behaviour
- Creating beauty from structure

Homeschooling allows children to hold multiple identities without being forced to choose too early. This is a strength, not a liability.

Working With Resistant or "Unmotivated" Learners

Few labels worry parents more than *unmotivated.*

When a child resists learning, avoids effort, or disengages entirely, it's tempting to assume the Element simply isn't there. But resistance usually means something else.

In my experience, resistance most often signals:

- Fear of failure
- Loss of autonomy
- Chronic mismatch between task and ability
- Exhaustion from constant evaluation

Children rarely lack motivation altogether. More often, they are motivated to protect themselves.

Before assuming a child has no Element, it's worth asking:

- When did learning begin to feel risky?
- What kinds of effort feel safe to them now?
- Where do they still show agency, even quietly?

For some learners, Element discovery begins not with passion, but with safety. Reducing pressure, rebuilding trust, and allowing genuine choice may need to come first.

Progress here is often slow --- and deeply meaningful.

- **Note for Diverse Learners:**
  For children recovering from school trauma, anxiety, or burnout, the Element may be hidden beneath layers of protective behaviours. The "deschooling" period --- where formal expectations are removed --- often needs to be longer for these learners. Trust that curiosity will re-emerge when safety is established.

When the Element Seems Impractical or Impossible

Sometimes parents do see the Element --- but feel stuck anyway.

What if your child's passion doesn't fit neatly into academic expectations?

What if it feels unrealistic, niche, or financially uncertain?

What if it doesn't look like "school" at all?

These concerns are understandable. They deserve honesty, not dismissal.

The purpose of Element discovery is not to lock a child into a career path. It is to anchor learning in meaning. Skills developed through meaningful work --- focus, problem-solving, communication, persistence --- transfer far more broadly than content learnt without engagement.

A child whose Element is storytelling can develop literacy, history, psychology, and ethics.

A child drawn to games can develop systems thinking, probability, design, and collaboration.

A child absorbed in animals can explore biology, data collection, advocacy, and writing.

The question is not whether the Element is practical.

The question is how to build learning pathways that honour it while expanding capability.

That is a design problem --- not a dead end.

A Reassuring Perspective

Some children find their Element early.
Some find it late.
Some revisit and revise it many times.
All of these paths are valid.

If you cannot see your child's Element yet, your work is not on hold. Observation, exploration, listening, and patience are not placeholders --- they are the work.

The Element does not require urgency.

It requires attention.

In the next chapter, we'll turn towards action --- exploring how to design Learning Expeditions that support curiosity even when the Element is still emerging, and that deepen engagement when it begins to show itself.

Because learning doesn't wait for certainty --- and neither should you.

Element Discovery
– at a Glance –

A simple guide to help you find where
your child's aptitudes and passions meet.

1 Observe Without Agenda

- Notice flow states
- Watch voluntary practice
- Jot it down—no conclusions yet

Pay attention before you interpret.

2 Offer a Low-Stakes Exploration Buffet

- Expose them to many experiences
- Keep it short and pressure-free
- Let "no thanks" count as data

Exploration works best without expectations.

3 Listen to Their Questions

- Follow curiosity, not completion
- Notice repeating questions
- Look for problems they love thinking about

Questions reveal depth.

4 Find the Through-Line

- Look for patterns across interests
- Notice how aptitude and passion overlap.

Common Mistakes:

- Jumping to conclusions
- Turning every curiosity into a lesson
- Labeling too early ("engineer","artist, "writer")
- Looking for answers instead of noting patterns

Element discovery unfolds in its own time.

You are not trying to decide who your child
will become – you are learning how they learn best.

Element discovery is a process, not a single insight. This image brings
together the four overlapping practices that help patterns emerge over
time

Chapter 4: Beyond the Obvious --- Hidden Elements

One of the reasons Element discovery feels elusive is that it rarely announces itself in tidy, school-approved forms.

Parents often expect the Element to look like a subject: maths, writing, science, art. But for many children --- especially those learning outside traditional classrooms --- the Element shows up first as a way of engaging, not a topic.

This chapter is about learning to see beneath the surface of what your child is doing, so you don't miss what's actually developing.

Underlying Skills vs. Surface Interests

It's easy to focus on what a child is doing.

They're drawing.
They're gaming.
They're building things.
They're telling stories.

But the Element usually lives one layer deeper --- in *how* the child is thinking, not just what they're interacting with.

Two children may appear to share the same interest while engaging in fundamentally different ways.

For example:

- One child draws to decorate; another draws to communicate ideas
- One child reads for comfort; another reads to analyse characters
- One child builds to follow instructions; another builds to improve systems

The activity is the same. The Element is not.

Homeschooling gives parents a rare advantage here: you get to witness process, not just product. You see how ideas form, where frustration appears, and what keeps a child returning.

When identifying the Element, ask yourself:

- What mental muscles does my child use most naturally here?
- What seems to energise them inside the activity?
- What part would they miss most if it were taken away?

The answers often point towards an underlying skill set that crosses many domains.

The "Minecraft Trap": What's Really at Work?

Few examples create more confusion --- or more parental guilt --- than Minecraft.

On the surface, it looks like a game. Or worse, "just screen time." Parents worry they're allowing something unproductive to crowd out "real learning."

But Minecraft is rarely the Element.

It is the environment.

What matters is what your child is doing inside it.

Some children use Minecraft to:

- Design and refine complex structures
- Experiment with cause-and-effect systems
- Collaborate, negotiate, and lead others
- Recreate historical or imagined worlds
- Optimise processes and resource flows

Others play briefly, casually, or repetitively without much engagement. Both experiences are valid --- but they signal different things.

Instead of asking, *Should I allow this?*, try asking:

- What keeps them coming back?
- What are they trying to improve?
- What frustrates them --- and how do they respond?
- Do they plan, revise, or explain their thinking?

Minecraft becomes a trap only when we stop at the surface and fail to interpret what's underneath.

Used thoughtfully, it can be a diagnostic window into a child's Element --- not a distraction from it.

Cross-Domain Elements: When It's Not About the Subject

Many children do not organise their interests around school subjects at all.

Instead, their Element lives in cross-domain capacities --- ways of thinking and creating that apply everywhere.

Here are three common examples.

Visual-Spatial Thinkers

These children think in images, patterns, and relationships in space. They may struggle with linear explanations but excel at:

- Design and layout
- Mapping and modelling
- Geometry, architecture, and engineering concepts
- Visual storytelling and illustration

Their Element may express itself through art, building, animation, or navigation --- but the underlying strength is spatial reasoning.

Narrative Thinkers

Narrative thinkers make sense of the world through story. They are drawn to:

- Characters and motivation
- Conflict and resolution
- History as lived experience
- Ethics, relationships, and identity

They may love writing --- or resist it entirely --- yet still be deeply engaged in storytelling through conversation, play, or imagination. The Element here is not writing itself, but meaning-making through narrative.

Systems Thinkers

These children are fascinated by how parts interact. They notice patterns, inefficiencies, and leverage points. You'll see this in:

- Games and simulations
- Coding and logic puzzles
- Organising collections or rules
- Asking "What would happen if...?"

Their Element may show up through maths, science, gaming, or strategy --- but the core strength is systems thinking, not any single subject.

Recognising cross-domain Elements helps parents stop searching for a perfect curricular match and start designing learning experiences that honour how a child thinks.

Why This Matters

When parents misidentify the Element, they often:

- Push children into mismatched instruction
- Miss transferable strengths
- Underestimate learning already happening

When parents see beneath the surface, something shifts.

Activities stop feeling like distractions.
Interests stop needing justification.
Learning starts to feel coherent --- even when it's unconventional.

The Element doesn't always announce itself with clarity. Sometimes it whispers through patterns, preferences, and persistence.

Your job is not to make it louder.

Your job is to learn how to listen better.

Case Study: Looking Past the Blocks

At first, Noah's parents were uneasy.

Noah was eleven and could spend hours in Minecraft. He talked about it constantly. He sketched designs for builds in the margins of notebooks. When asked what he was doing, his answers sounded vague: "Just working on something."

To his parents, it didn't look like learning. It looked repetitive. Isolated. Digital.

They tried limiting time, redirecting towards "more educational" activities, and suggesting structured alternatives. None of it worked. Noah complied briefly, then drifted back.

Eventually, instead of intervening, his parents decided to observe.

They noticed that Noah didn't wander aimlessly in the game. He planned. He experimented. He rebuilt. He became frustrated when systems didn't work efficiently and visibly satisfied when they did.

When playing with others, he naturally took on a coordinating role --- explaining ideas, assigning tasks, and negotiating changes. When something failed, he didn't quit. He revised.

What changed things was a single question.

Instead of asking, *Why are you still playing this?* his parent asked:

What are you trying to improve right now?

Noah lit up.

He explained how resource flow could be optimised, how redstone circuits could be simplified, how certain designs reduced wasted effort. He talked about trade-offs. Constraints. Elegance.

The Element wasn't Minecraft.

It was systems thinking.

Once his parents saw that, learning shifted. Game design books replaced time limits. Logic puzzles appeared. Coding became interesting. Maths stopped being abstract when it described systems Noah already understood intuitively.

Minecraft hadn't been the problem.

It had been the window.

Reflection for Parents

If you took away the surface activity, what thinking would remain?

That question --- asked honestly --- often reveals more than hours of correction ever could.

- **Note for Diverse Learners:**
  For autistic children and others with intense interests, the "special interest" is often the most reliable pathway to the Element. Rather than trying to broaden interests prematurely, lean into the depth. The cognitive patterns developed through deep engagement transfer to new domains when the child is ready.

PART II:

Designing Learning

Bridge: From Discovery to Design

You've spent time observing. You've noticed patterns. Perhaps you've even identified a through-line in how your child engages with the world.

Now comes the question that matters most:

What do we do with this understanding?

This is where many families stumble --- not because they lack insight, but because the gap between *noticing* and *designing* feels vast. Traditional curriculum doesn't fit anymore, but building something from scratch feels overwhelming.

This is exactly where Learning Expeditions come in.

A Learning Expedition is not:

- A unit study with predetermined endpoints
- A project assigned by you and completed by your child
- A way to "cover" subjects more creatively

A Learning Expedition is:

- An extended investigation driven by genuine curiosity
- A journey where academic skills emerge because they're needed
- A structure flexible enough to honour your child's Element while building rigour

The next two chapters will show you how expeditions work and how to design your first one. But before we begin, let's address the elephant in the room.

"But What About Maths and English?"

This is the question I hear most often when parents first encounter the expedition model.

This sounds wonderful, but how do I make sure they're learning to read, write, and calculate properly?

It's a legitimate concern. And the answer matters deeply.

Core literacies are not separate from expeditions --- they are the tools that make expeditions possible.

Reading happens because children need to research.
Writing happens because ideas need to be captured and shared.
Mathematics happens because problems need to be measured, compared, or analysed.

In Part III, we'll explore how to ensure these foundational skills develop with intention. For now, hold this principle:

Skills learnt in context stick longer and feel purposeful.

When a child learns to calculate percentages because they're tracking plant growth in their garden expedition, the mathematics becomes meaningful. When they learn persuasive writing because they're advocating for a community issue they care about, the writing becomes powerful.

This doesn't mean we never teach skills directly. Sometimes direct instruction is exactly what's needed --- and we'll talk about when and how in Chapter 8.

But it does mean we stop treating subjects as isolated checkboxes and start seeing them as interconnected tools for understanding the world.

The Architecture of Deep Learning

Before we dive into expedition design, it helps to understand what makes learning "stick."

Research on learning consistently shows that knowledge becomes durable when it is:

1. **Connected** to prior understanding
2. **Applied** in meaningful contexts
3. **Revisited** multiple times over extended periods
4. **Shared** with authentic audiences

Traditional schooling often fails on all four counts. Content is fragmented, application is artificial, coverage happens once, and "sharing" means handing work to a teacher who already knows the answer.

Learning Expeditions reverse this entirely.

They create natural conditions for connection (interdisciplinary by design), application (anchored in real problems), revision (sustained over weeks or months), and authentic sharing (public products for real audiences).

This is why expeditions work --- not because they're more fun (though they often are), but because they align with how human beings actually learn.

What Makes This Different From What You've Tried Before

If you've already experimented with project-based learning, unit studies, or interest-led education, you might be thinking: *Haven't I already done this?*

Maybe. But probably not quite like this.

The Learning Expedition model is distinguished by three non-negotiables:

1. Real-World Anchor Problems
Not "topics" or "themes," but genuine questions or challenges that matter beyond the homeschool.

2. Sustained Inquiry
Not a week-long project, but an extended investigation (typically 4-12 weeks) that allows for depth, revision, and genuine intellectual growth.

3. Public Accountability
Not work completed for parental approval, but products or presentations shared with authentic audiences who care about the outcome.

These three elements transform casual exploration into rigorous learning.

And here's the part that matters most for homeschooling families:

You don't need to know everything. You just need to design the conditions where learning wants to happen.

In the chapters that follow, you'll learn exactly how to do that.

Chapter 5: What Is a Learning Expedition?

Once parents begin to recognise a child's Element --- or even just the beginnings of one --- the next question usually follows quickly:

What do we do with this?

How do curiosity, aptitude, and interest turn into something that feels like real education rather than a collection of disconnected activities?

This is where Learning Expeditions come in.

A Learning Expedition is not a curriculum and not a single project. It is a way of organising learning so that depth, meaning, and rigour grow naturally out of a child's curiosity --- without sacrificing structure or intention.

The Expeditionary Learning Model, Explained Simply

The idea of Learning Expeditions comes from the Expeditionary Learning (EL) school model, where students learn through extended investigations of real-world problems. Rather than moving quickly from topic to topic, EL schools organise learning around big questions, authentic work, and public outcomes.

In these environments, students don't just learn *about* something --- they learn *through* it.

An expedition might last weeks or even months. During that time, students read, write, research, calculate, design, revise, and present --- not because these skills are assigned, but because the work demands them.

For homeschoolers, this model is powerful because it mirrors how learning actually happens outside of school. Adults don't learn in isolated subjects. We learn when we're trying to understand something that matters to us.

A Learning Expedition gives children that same experience.

How Learning Expeditions Differ From Other Approaches

Many homeschooling families already use projects, unit studies, or unschooling. Learning Expeditions may look similar on the surface, but the intentional structure is what makes the difference.

Projects

Projects are usually short-term and outcome-focused. They often begin with an assignment and end with a product.

Expeditions are longer and enquiry-driven. The product matters --- but it grows out of sustained thinking, revision, and discovery.

Unit Studies

Unit studies group subjects around a theme. Whilst this creates coherence, the learning is often still pre-planned and content-driven.

Expeditions are problem-centred. The questions evolve as understanding deepens, and learning pathways adapt along the way.

Unschooling

Unschooling values autonomy and trust in natural learning, which many families find freeing and effective.

Learning Expeditions share this respect for curiosity but add design. They provide enough structure to ensure depth, challenge, and skill development --- without returning to rigid schedules or artificial benchmarks.

In short, Learning Expeditions sit at the intersection of freedom and form.

The Anatomy of a Successful Learning Expedition

Whilst no two expeditions look exactly the same, effective ones share a common structure. Think of these elements not as requirements, but as support beams.

1. A Real-World Anchor Problem

Every expedition begins with a problem, question, or challenge that feels real --- not hypothetical or performative.

Examples might include:

- How can we design a shelter that stays cool without electricity?
- What makes a game fair --- and how could we redesign one?
- How does misinformation spread, and how can people recognise it?
- How could we tell the story of this place in a way others would care about?

The anchor problem gives learning a reason to exist. It answers the child's unspoken question: *Why does this matter?*

- **Note for Diverse Learners:**
  For children with anxiety or perfectionism, the "realness" of anchor problems can feel overwhelming. Start with lower-stakes questions where failure is safe and expected. "How could we improve our backyard for birds?" is less intimidating than "How can we solve climate change?"

2. Sustained Inquiry (Weeks to Months)

Learning Expeditions unfold over time.

Instead of racing towards completion, children linger. They revisit ideas. They revise their thinking. New questions emerge, and old assumptions fall away.

This sustained enquiry allows for:

- Deeper understanding
- Skill growth through repeated use
- Productive struggle
- Intellectual maturity

Depth, not speed, is the goal.

3. Interdisciplinary Integration

In an expedition, subjects stop being separate.

Reading is needed to research.
Writing is needed to communicate ideas.
Maths is needed to measure, analyse, or compare.
Science, history, art, and technology appear as tools rather than tasks.

This integration mirrors real life --- and it often reveals strengths that traditional subject divisions hide.

Children begin to see learning as a system, not a checklist.

4. A Public Product or Presentation

A defining feature of Expeditionary Learning is the public product --- something shared beyond the immediate family.

This might be:

- A presentation to community members
- A performance
- A published piece of writing
- A model, prototype, or exhibition
- Teaching others what they've learnt

Public work raises the stakes in a healthy way. It encourages care, clarity, and revision --- not through pressure, but through purpose.

Children often work harder when they know their work will matter to someone else.

5. Character Challenges Built In

Learning Expeditions develop more than knowledge.

Because the work is sustained and meaningful, children naturally encounter challenges that build character:

- Perseverance when ideas don't work
- Responsibility to a group or audience
- Courage to share unfinished thinking
- Humility to revise and improve

These traits are not taught through lectures. They emerge through experience.

This is one of the most overlooked strengths of the expedition model.

Why Learning Expeditions Work So Well for Homeschooling

Homeschooling allows for flexibility, personalisation, and responsiveness --- qualities that Learning Expeditions depend on.

Parents are not expected to be content experts. Their role is to:

- Help frame meaningful questions
- Provide resources and opportunities
- Encourage reflection and revision
- Support challenge without rescuing

In this model, learning becomes a shared journey rather than a transaction.

Children are not completing schoolwork.
They are doing work worth completing.

Case Study: The Bridge That Wouldn't Hold

It started with a walk.

On the way home from the library, twelve-year-old Maya stopped at a small footbridge near their neighbourhood park. She leant over the rail and asked why it shook so much when people crossed.

Her parent didn't have an answer. Instead of moving on, they paused.

That evening, the question came back:

How do bridges actually work?

There was no lesson plan. No timeline. Just curiosity.

Over the next few weeks, the question grew. Maya began noticing bridges everywhere --- on bike paths, in books, in videos. She sketched designs at the kitchen table and tested them with cardboard and string. Some collapsed immediately. Others held, briefly.

When her designs failed, she adjusted them. When she didn't understand why something worked, she looked it up.

Maths appeared when she needed to measure. Physics appeared when structures bent or broke. Writing appeared when she began keeping notes so she wouldn't forget what she'd tried.

Her parent helped find resources, suggested a local engineer to email, and asked questions that slowed Maya's thinking just enough to deepen it.

Eventually, Maya decided to build a small model bridge sturdy enough for her younger sibling's toy cars. When it was finished, she presented it --- along with sketches, explanations, and failed attempts --- to family members one evening after dinner.

She was nervous. She spoke carefully. She revised her explanation when questions came.

The bridge held.

What mattered most wasn't the model itself. It was the way Maya had learnt to persist, revise, explain, and take pride in work that hadn't existed a month earlier.

No one ever said, "We are doing a Learning Expedition."

But that's exactly what it was.

A Thought to Carry Forward

Learning Expeditions don't begin with certainty.

They begin with attention.

And they don't end with answers --- they end with capacity.

In the next chapter, we'll explore how to design Learning Expeditions that grow naturally out of a child's emerging Element --- turning curiosity into sustained, meaningful learning.

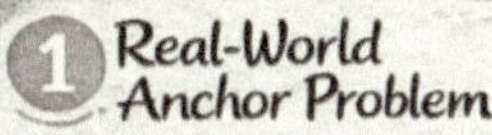

As an expedition unfolds, structure and flexibility work side by side. This visual shows how real questions, interdisciplinary learning, and character growth are woven into the process.

Chapter 6: Designing Your First Learning Expedition

By now, Learning Expeditions may feel inspiring --- but also a little intimidating.

If you're thinking, *This sounds meaningful, but I'm not sure I know how to design one*, you're in exactly the right place. Designing your first expedition is not about getting everything right. It's about starting small, staying responsive, and letting clarity emerge through action.

This chapter will walk you through that process --- step by step.

Start Smaller Than You Think

One of the most common mistakes parents make is assuming that a "real" Learning Expedition has to be large, polished, or long.

It doesn't.

Your first expedition might last a week. It might stay messy. It might change direction halfway through. All of that still counts.

A good first expedition:

- Grows out of a real question
- Has room to deepen
- Leaves you and your child wanting to try again

That's it.

Momentum matters more than scope.

Step 1: Choose a Question, Not a Topic

Topics are broad. Questions are active.

Instead of:

- Ancient Egypt
- Weather
- Writing stories

Try:

- How did ancient people solve everyday problems without modern tools?
- Why do some storms cause more damage than others?
- What makes a story stay with someone long after it ends?

Questions invite investigation. Topics invite coverage.

When in doubt, listen for the question your child keeps circling back to --- sometimes without realising it.

Where Questions Come From

Expedition questions can emerge from:

- **Repeated curiosity**: "Why do you keep asking about that?"
- **Frustration**: "I wish this worked differently"
- **The boredom test**: What captures attention when nothing is required?
- **The Element intersection**: Where aptitude meets passion
- **Current events**: Something happening in your community or the world
- **Everyday problems**: Something that genuinely needs solving

The best first expeditions often start with the smallest, most honest questions.

Step 2: Design for Depth, Not Coverage

Traditional schooling often rewards moving on quickly. Learning Expeditions do the opposite.

Depth comes from:

- Revisiting ideas
- Testing and revising thinking
- Sitting with confusion
- Asking better questions over time

You don't need to plan everything in advance. Instead, plan for pauses:

- Time to reflect
- Time to notice what's emerging
- Time to ask, "What's the next right step?"

Depth is not something you schedule. It's something you allow.

The "One Layer Deeper" Principle

When you think you've explored enough, go one layer deeper.

If your child has researched how bridges work, ask: "Could you design one that would work in our garden?"

If they've written a story, ask: "What would happen if you told it from a different character's perspective?"

If they've built a model, ask: "How could you make it more efficient?"

This principle prevents shallow completion and invites genuine mastery.

Step 3: Gather Resources Lightly

You don't need a stack of books or a curated syllabus.

Start with just enough:

- One or two accessible resources
- A way to observe or experiment
- A person or place connected to the question

As the expedition unfolds, new needs will become obvious. Let the work itself tell you what resources belong next.

This keeps learning responsive rather than pre-loaded --- and prevents burnout for both parent and child.

Resource Types to Consider

- **Primary sources**: Original documents, interviews, direct observation
- **Expert voices**: Local professionals, online specialists, documentary makers
- **Hands-on materials**: Building supplies, art materials, tools for experimentation
- **Digital tools**: Educational videos, simulation software, research databases
- **Community connections**: Libraries, maker spaces, museums, nature reserves

Remember: resources are not the curriculum. They are the scaffolding.

Step 4: Let Skills Emerge Naturally

One of the quiet strengths of Learning Expeditions is that academic skills appear because they're needed.

Writing happens because ideas need to be captured or shared.
Maths happens because something needs to be measured or compared.
Reading happens because understanding requires context.

Instead of asking, *How do I make sure we cover everything?*, try asking:

- What skill would make this work stronger?
- What does my child need to learn next to keep going?

Skills learnt in context stick longer --- and feel purposeful.

When Direct Instruction Belongs

Sometimes you'll notice your child needs a skill they don't have yet. This is where brief, targeted instruction fits naturally:

"To answer this question, you need to understand percentages. Let's spend twenty minutes learning how they work."

"Your explanation would be clearer with better paragraph structure. Can I show you a technique?"

Direct teaching isn't banned from expeditions --- it's just-in-time rather than just-in-case.

Step 5: Plan for a Share, Not a Performance

Early on, it helps to imagine how learning might be shared --- but without locking it in.

A "share" can be simple:

- Explaining learning to someone else
- Showing a model or drawing
- Teaching a concept to a sibling
- Answering questions at the dinner table
- Creating a small display or demonstration

Public products don't need to impress. They need to clarify thinking.

The goal is not polish.
The goal is meaning.

- **Note for Diverse Learners:**
For children with social anxiety or presentation fear, "public" can start very small --- sharing with one trusted person, recording a video instead of presenting live, or creating a written guide. The accountability matters more than the audience size.

Step 6: Expect Resistance --- and Welcome It

At some point, your child may say:

"This is hard."
"I don't know what to do next."
"I don't want to fix it again."

These moments are not signs of failure. They are signs that learning is real.

Your role is not to remove the challenge --- but to help your child stay with it:

- Ask what feels stuck
- Break the problem into smaller parts
- Normalise revision and uncertainty
- Share your own experiences with difficulty

This is where character grows --- not through lectures, but through experience.

The "Productive Struggle" Window

There's a sweet spot between "too easy" (boredom) and "too hard" (shutdown). This is where real learning happens.

Signs you're in the productive struggle window:

- Frustration is present but manageable
- Your child returns to the problem voluntarily
- Small breakthroughs feel genuinely satisfying
- Effort feels worthwhile, not pointless

If your child shuts down completely, the challenge is too big. Scale back. If they're coasting without effort, increase complexity.

Step 7: Build in Reflection Points

Learning doesn't become meaningful until it's reflected upon.

Build in natural pause points:

- **Mid-expedition check-in**: "What have you learnt so far? What surprised you?"
- **Problem-solving moments**: "That didn't work. What do you think went wrong?"
- **Before the share**: "What's the most important thing you want people to understand?"
- **After completion**: "What would you do differently next time?"

These conversations turn experience into insight.

Common First-Expedition Missteps (and Reframes)

"It doesn't look like school."
Good. It's not meant to.

"We didn't finish."
Learning isn't measured by completion --- it's measured by growth.

"It changed direction."
That's responsiveness, not failure.

"I don't think we did enough."
Enough is defined by engagement, not volume.

"My child lost interest halfway through."
That's valuable information. What did you learn about their Element?

"I did too much of the work."
Next time, do less. Let struggle be their teacher.

A Template for Your First Expedition

Use the Learning Expedition Starter in the Appendix, but here's a
simplified version:

1. **The Spark**: What question is your child genuinely curious
   about?
2. **Why Now**: What makes this question meaningful right now?
3. **Possible Directions**: What might you explore? (List 3-5
   possibilities)
4. **Skills That Might Emerge**: What could your child learn
   through this? (Don't force --- just anticipate)
5. **Possible Share**: How might this learning be shown to others?
6. **Time Frame**: How long might this take? (Always flexible)

That's all you need to begin.

A Reassuring Truth

Your first Learning Expedition will not be your best one.

And that's exactly the point.

Each expedition builds confidence --- for you and your child. You learn how to notice, when to step in, when to step back, and how to trust the process.

Learning Expeditions are not about control.
They're about designing conditions where learning wants to happen.

In the next chapter, we'll look at how to reflect, adjust, and build momentum --- so each expedition informs the next, and learning becomes a sustainable rhythm rather than a series of experiments.

Because the goal isn't to run one perfect expedition.

It's to create a life where learning keeps unfolding.

Chapter 7: Reflection, Revision, and Momentum

Learning Expeditions don't end when the activity stops.

They end when meaning is made.

Without reflection, even rich learning can feel fleeting. With it, families begin to see patterns, build confidence, and create momentum that carries into the next expedition naturally.

This chapter is about learning how to pause well, so learning can keep moving forward.

Why Reflection Matters More Than Completion

In traditional schooling, completion is often treated as the goal. Assignments are finished, units are closed, and learning moves on --- whether understanding is deep or not.

Learning Expeditions work differently.

Because expeditions are open-ended, reflective pauses are what turn experience into insight.

Reflection helps children:

- Recognise their own growth
- Understand how they learn
- Build confidence in persistence
- See connections across experiences

For parents, reflection offers clarity. It answers the quiet questions:

Did this matter? Did we actually learn anything? Should we do this again?

Reflection is how those questions become grounded in evidence rather than anxiety.

Reflecting With Your Child (Without Turning It Into a Test)

Reflection doesn't need to be formal or written --- especially at first. It works best as conversation, drawing, storytelling, or quiet noticing.

Good reflection questions are:

- Open-ended
- Curious, not evaluative
- Focused on process rather than results

Try questions like:

- What part of this felt most interesting to you?
- What was harder than you expected?
- What changed in your thinking?
- What would you do differently next time?
- What are you still wondering about?

You're not looking for "right" answers. You're helping your child develop metacognition --- the ability to think about their own thinking.

That skill alone is worth the expedition.

Reflection Formats That Work

Not every child processes verbally. Try:

- **Sketchnoting**: Drawing what they learnt with labels and arrows
- **Before/After thinking**: "What did you think at the start? What do you think now?"
- **Teaching someone else**: The best test of understanding
- **Photo documentation**: Looking back through images of the process
- **"Best moment / hardest moment"**: A simple two-question frame

Match the reflection tool to your child's natural communication style.

Reflecting as a Parent

Your reflection matters too.

After an expedition --- or even partway through --- take a few minutes to ask yourself:

- When was my child most engaged?
- When did resistance show up, and why?
- Which supports helped? Which got in the way?
- What surprised me about how my child learnt?
- What would I do differently next time?

This kind of reflection helps you refine your role. Over time, you'll notice yourself intervening less urgently, asking better questions, and trusting the process more deeply.

That confidence compounds.

The Parent Observation Journal

Keep a simple notebook where you jot down:

- Moments of deep engagement
- Questions your child asked
- Skills that emerged naturally
- Where you struggled as the facilitator
- Ideas for next expeditions

This becomes your curriculum design document --- not something prescribed, but something discovered.

Revision: Letting Learning Continue Its Work

Revision is often misunderstood as fixing mistakes.

In Learning Expeditions, revision is about growth, not correction.

Children revise ideas, models, explanations, and plans as they learn more. Sometimes revision happens during the expedition. Sometimes it happens later --- when a new experience sheds light on an old one.

It's okay if revision looks subtle:

- A clearer explanation
- A refined question
- A more thoughtful approach next time

Revision means learning is alive, not finished.

Creating a Revision Culture

In many homes, "revision" carries shame --- it means you got it wrong the first time.

In expedition-based learning, revision is expected and celebrated:

- "Your first attempt showed you what doesn't work. That's progress."
- "Now that you understand more, how would you improve this?"
- "Professional writers revise ten times. This is your second draft --- you're right on track."

When revision becomes normal, fear of failure shrinks.

Knowing When an Expedition Is "Done"

One of the hardest parts for parents is knowing when to stop.

There is no perfect ending point. But expeditions often reach a natural close when:

- Curiosity begins to fade
- Questions have shifted elsewhere
- The work feels complete for now
- Energy moves towards something new

Ending an expedition doesn't mean abandoning it. It means trusting that learning has done what it needed to do at this stage.

You can always return.

The "Shelf It" Option

Some expeditions don't end --- they pause.

Your child might:

- Run out of energy before reaching their original goal
- Lack skills or resources to continue right now
- Need time for ideas to mature

That's fine. Put it on the shelf. Come back in three months. Many of the best expeditions are revisited after growth elsewhere makes them newly possible.

Building Momentum Into the Next Expedition

Reflection often reveals the seeds of what comes next.

A comment like:

"I liked explaining it to people."
"I wish I had more time to improve this."
"Now I'm curious about something else."

These are invitations.

Rather than planning the next expedition from scratch, you can often follow these threads forward. Momentum builds when learning feels continuous rather than segmented.

Over time, families develop a rhythm:

Observe → Explore → Reflect → Adjust → Begin Again

This rhythm becomes more important than any individual expedition.

The Expedition Cycle

Think of your homeschool year not as a linear progression through content, but as a series of expeditions with reflective pauses between them.

A typical year might include:

- 3-5 major expeditions (4-12 weeks each)
- 2-3 minor explorations (1-2 weeks)
- Flexible time for skill-building, rest, and unstructured play

Between expeditions, use reflection to:

- Celebrate growth
- Identify skill gaps
- Notice emerging interests
- Plan (lightly) for what's next

This creates sustainable rhythm instead of perpetual hustle.

- **Note for Diverse Learners:**
Children with ADHD or anxiety often need longer transition periods between expeditions. Build in "reset time" where expectations are minimal and energy can restore. This isn't lost time --- it's essential for sustainable learning.

A Final Perspective

Learning Expeditions are not about producing impressive work.

They are about shaping learners who:

- Notice deeply
- Persist thoughtfully
- Reflect honestly
- Revise willingly

When reflection and revision become normal parts of learning, children stop fearing mistakes and start seeing themselves as capable thinkers.

And parents stop asking, *Are we doing enough?*

They start seeing that learning is happening --- again and again.

Closing Thought

Learning doesn't move in straight lines.

But when you pause to reflect, you can always see how far you've come.

The Learning Expedition Cycle:
From Curiosity to Deep Learning

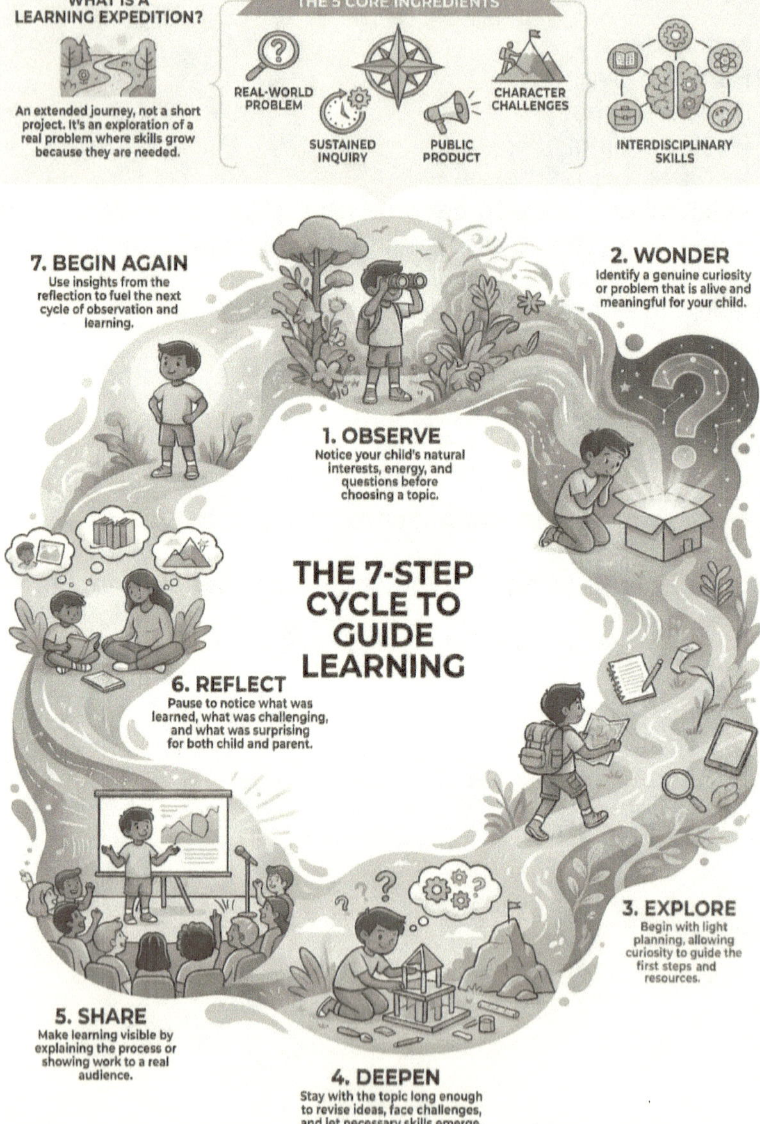

Learning does not move in straight lines. This cycle reflects the ongoing rhythm of observation, exploration, reflection, and renewal that guides each new expedition.

PART III:

Sustaining the Work

Chapter 8: Core Literacies --- The Tools That Make Everything Else Possible

Here's the question I'm asked most often when parents first encounter Learning Expeditions:

"This sounds wonderful, but what about maths and English? How do I make sure my child can actually read, write, and calculate?"

It's a legitimate concern. And it deserves a thorough answer.

This chapter exists to show you how core literacies --- reading, writing, and mathematics --- develop within expedition-based learning without sacrificing rigour or depth.

The Myth of Separation

Traditional schooling taught us that subjects are separate. That maths happens during maths time, writing happens during English, and reading happens with readers.

This separation is artificial.

In real life, literacy and numeracy are tools we use to solve problems, communicate ideas, and understand the world. They don't exist in isolation --- they exist in service of meaningful work.

Learning Expeditions honour this reality.

Core literacies are not separate from expeditions --- they are the tools that make expeditions possible.

How Reading Develops Through Expeditions

Reading is not a subject. It's a gateway.

When children are genuinely curious about something, reading becomes the obvious path to understanding.

What Reading Looks Like in Expeditions

- **Research**: "I need to find out how ancient Romans built aqueducts"
- **Comparison**: "What do different sources say about this?"
- **Instructions**: "How do I build the model the right way?"
- **Context**: "I need to understand the history before I can explain this"

The difference is profound: children aren't reading to prove they can read. They're reading because they need to know something.

Teaching Reading Skills Within Expeditions

This doesn't mean you never teach reading directly. Sometimes explicit instruction is exactly what's needed:

- "To research this question, you need to skim for relevant information. Let me show you how."
- "This text is complex. Let's read it together and discuss what it means."
- "You're ready for more challenging material. Let's practice strategies for tackling difficult texts."

The instruction is just-in-time, not just-in-case.

For Emerging Readers

If your child is still developing foundational reading skills, you can:

- Read expedition-related texts aloud together
- Use audiobooks and documentaries as alternate input sources
- Pair image-heavy resources with text
- Celebrate every instance where reading serves their curiosity

Motivation to read grows when reading has obvious purpose.

How Writing Develops Through Expeditions

Writing is thinking made visible.

In expeditions, children write because they have something worth saying --- and someone worth saying it to.

What Writing Looks Like in Expeditions

- **Recording observations**: Field notes, sketches with captions, journals
- **Explaining thinking**: "Here's how I solved this problem"
- **Communicating findings**: Letters, reports, presentations, guides
- **Persuading others**: Proposals, arguments, advocacy
- **Storytelling**: Historical fiction, creative narratives based on research

Writing becomes a tool for clarifying thought, not a performance for grades.

Teaching Writing Skills Within Expeditions

Again, direct instruction has its place:

- "Your explanation would be clearer with topic sentences. Let me show you."
- "You're making an argument here. Arguments need evidence. Let's talk about how to structure that."
- "Your audience needs context. What background information should you include?"

The difference is that children can see why these skills matter --- immediately.

Writing as Process, Not Product

In expeditions, children experience writing as:

- Drafting and revision (because the work matters)
- Feedback from real audiences (not just teacher comments)
- Multiple purposes and formats (not just essays)

This builds far more versatile writers than isolated grammar exercises ever could.

How Mathematics Develops Through Expeditions

This is often the hardest for parents to trust.

We've been taught that maths is a linear sequence of skills to be mastered in order. Miss one step, and everything after fails.

Eddie Woo's teaching shows us something different: **mathematics is sense-making**. It's pattern recognition, logical reasoning, and problem-solving applied to the world.

When children encounter real problems that require mathematical thinking, they develop both skills and intuition.

What Mathematics Looks Like in Expeditions

- **Measurement and estimation**: "How much material do we need?"
- **Data collection and analysis**: "Let's track this over time and look for patterns"
- **Proportional reasoning**: "If we scale this up, what changes?"
- **Financial literacy**: "How much will this cost? Is it worth it?"
- **Probability and risk**: "What's likely to happen? How do we know?"
- **Geometry and spatial reasoning**: Building, designing, mapping
- **Statistical thinking**: Interpreting information, questioning claims

Mathematics appears as a tool for understanding, not an isolated skill set.

Teaching Maths Skills Within Expeditions

Yes, sometimes children need direct instruction in mathematical concepts:

- "To answer this question, you need to understand percentages. Let's learn how they work."
- "You're noticing patterns in your data. That's algebra --- let me show you how to express it formally."
- "Your design would be stronger if you understood ratios. Let's explore that."

The key difference: **children can see why they need the maths**. It's not arbitrary. It's purposeful.

When to Use Formal Maths Resources

Some families supplement expeditions with structured maths programs (Khan Academy, Beast Academy, Life of Fred, etc.). This can work beautifully if:

- **The program is used as a tool, not the centre of learning**: Maths time supports expedition work, not the reverse
- **Concepts connect to expedition work when possible**: "You're learning multiplication because you'll need it for your garden design"
- **Your child maintains agency over pacing**: They can move faster or slower based on understanding
- **It doesn't crowd out expedition time**: 20-30 minutes daily maximum
- **Mistakes are treated as learning, not failure**: The focus is on understanding, not performance

There's no single right answer. Some children thrive with formal maths structure. Others develop mathematical thinking entirely through applied problems.

Trust your observation of your child.

Eddie Woo's Insight: Mathematics as Social Power

One of Eddie Woo's most compelling arguments is that mathematical literacy is fundamentally about power and agency.

People who understand numbers can:

- Question claims made with statistics
- Understand their own finances
- Make informed decisions about risk
- See through manipulative marketing
- Participate fully in civic life

This is why mathematics matters --- not because you might need algebra in your job, but because mathematical thinking is democratic participation.

Frame mathematics this way for your child: "We're learning this so no one can trick you with numbers."

That motivation is far more powerful than "You'll need this for the test."

The "Just-in-Time" Principle

The core principle for all three literacies is this:

Teach skills when they're needed, not when they might be needed someday.

This doesn't mean waiting until a child is behind. It means watching for teachable moments:

- The moment frustration signals a missing skill
- The moment curiosity makes new learning relevant
- The moment a challenge demands deeper understanding

These moments create what educators call "desirable difficulty" --- the perfect conditions for lasting learning.

What "Just-in-Time" Looks Like in Practice

Example 1: Reading During a bird-watching expedition, your child wants to identify species but struggles with field guide text.

Just-in-time moment: "These field guides use specific vocabulary. Let's learn how scientific descriptions work."

Example 2: Writing Your child wants to write to the city council about a playground issue but doesn't know how to structure a formal letter.

Just-in-time moment: "Letters like this follow a pattern. Let me show you how persuasive writing works."

Example 3: Mathematics Your child is designing a treehouse but their measurements keep producing structures that don't fit together.

Just-in-time moment: "You need to understand scale and proportion. Let's work on that now because you need it."

The difference is profound: skills aren't learnt in isolation and then hoped to transfer. They're learnt because the child can immediately see their power and purpose.

What About Skill Gaps?

Parents worry: *"What if my child reaches sixteen and can't write a formal essay because we've only done expedition work?"*

Here's what actually happens:

A child who has spent years:

- Reading for genuine purpose
- Writing to communicate real ideas
- Solving mathematical problems that matter

… can learn formal essay structure in a few focused sessions when it's needed (usually for university applications or standardised tests).

The foundation of literacy isn't format mastery. It's confidence with language, numbers, and ideas.

Skills transfer. Confidence transfers. Curiosity transfers.

Isolated drills rarely transfer at all.

The Research on Transfer

Studies of learning consistently show that:

- Skills learnt in isolation rarely apply to new contexts
- Skills learnt in meaningful contexts transfer broadly
- Motivation and confidence matter more than content coverage
- Deep understanding in narrow domains beats shallow exposure across many

Your child who has deeply engaged with mathematical thinking through designing a game has developed reasoning skills that will serve them across dozens of contexts.

Your child who has written extensively about topics they care about can learn any format quickly because they understand how to communicate effectively.

Trust the foundation you're building.

- **Note for Diverse Learners:**
  Children with dyslexia, dysgraphia, or dyscalculia may
  need explicit, structured intervention for foundational skills.
  This isn't a failure of the expedition model --- it's
  appropriate support. Many families successfully blend
  structured literacy programs (Orton-Gillingham, Barton
  Reading, Wilson Reading, etc.) with expedition learning.
  The expeditions provide motivation and meaning; the
  intervention provides tools and strategies. These
  approaches strengthen each other rather than compete.

A Practical Framework: The 80/20 Rule

Here's a sustainable approach many families find effective:

80% of learning time: Expedition-based, integrated, child-driven

20% of learning time: Targeted skill-building in areas that need
attention

This might look like:

Schedule Option 1:

- Monday, Wednesday, Friday mornings: Expedition work
- Tuesday, Thursday mornings: Focused literacy/numeracy skill
  development
- Afternoons: Flexible for research, exploration, documentation

Schedule Option 2:

- Mornings: Begin with 20-30 minutes of focused skill work
  (maths practice, writing mechanics, reading strategies)
- Rest of morning and afternoon: Expedition work where skills
  are applied

Schedule Option 3:

- Expeditions as the primary structure throughout the week
- One afternoon per week dedicated to addressing specific skill gaps identified during expedition work

The ratio isn't sacred. Some children need more structured literacy support. Others barely need any. Adjust based on your child's needs and your observations.

But remember: **the expedition work is developing literacy and numeracy too** --- just not in isolation.

Assessing Core Literacy Development

How do you know if it's working?

Traditional assessment looks at test scores and grade levels. Expedition-based assessment looks at capability and growth.

Watch for these signs:

Reading Development

✓ **Increasing complexity** of texts chosen voluntarily

✓ **Better comprehension** when discussing ideas

✓ **More sophisticated vocabulary** in speech and writing

✓ **Ability to locate and use information** independently

✓ **Critical evaluation** of sources and claims

✓ **Choosing to read** for pleasure and purpose

Writing Development

✓ **Longer, more detailed** written work

✓ **Clearer organisation** of ideas

✓ **Revision without prompting** ("Let me fix that")

✓ **Varied purposes and formats** (not just one kind of writing)

✓ **Voice emerging** (their personality shows in their writing)

✓ **Writing as thinking tool** ("Let me write this down to figure it out")

Mathematics Development

✓ **Spontaneous use** of mathematical thinking to solve problems

✓ **Questions that show numerical reasoning** ("What's the ratio?"
  "Is that actually bigger?")

✓ **Comfort with estimation** and approximation

✓ **Ability to explain mathematical thinking** clearly

✓ **Recognition of patterns** across different contexts

✓ **Confidence tackling new mathematical challenges**

These developmental markers matter far more than workbook pages completed or curriculum units finished.

When Formal Assessment Is Useful

Some families need or want formal assessment for various reasons:

Legal compliance: Some jurisdictions require standardised testing or portfolio review

External validation: Sometimes you need outside confirmation that learning is progressing

Identifying learning differences: Formal assessment can diagnose specific challenges that need support

Preparing for transitions: If your child might return to traditional school or needs test scores for programmes

Personal reassurance: Sometimes parents need objective measures to quiet their own anxieties

That's all fine. Formal assessment can coexist with expedition learning.

Using Standardised Tests Appropriately

If you use standardised tests:

Do:

- Contextualise results ("This measures one narrow skill set")
- Use results diagnostically ("This shows we should work on X")
- Recognise test-taking is its own skill
- Prepare specifically for test format
- Remember: one data point among many

Don't:

- Let test results define your child's worth or intelligence
- Reorganise your entire approach based on scores
- Compare to grade-level "norms" that assume traditional schooling
- Panic over weak areas that aren't actually priorities
- Use tests to "prove" homeschooling to doubters (you don't owe anyone that proof)

Just remember: **tests measure a narrow slice of competence**. They don't capture creativity, persistence, collaboration, ethical reasoning, problem-solving, or genuine understanding.

Use them as one data point among many --- never the only measure of learning.

Real Examples: How Core Literacies Develop

Let's return to our case studies to see this in practice.

Maya's Literacy Development (Visual-Spatial Learner)

Reading: By age 12, Maya was reading:

- Graphic novels and illustrated texts fluently
- Art history and biography
- Technical books about design and architecture
- Increasingly complex texts when they connected to visual thinking

Her parents worried initially because she didn't love chapter books. But her reading comprehension was excellent --- she just preferred certain formats. That's not a deficit; that's a preference.

Writing: Maya developed strong writing skills through:

- Character backstories and visual narratives
- Explanatory text for her artwork
- Research reports on architectural history
- Grant applications for art projects (age 14)

Her writing was vivid and precise --- shaped by her visual thinking.

Mathematics: Maya encountered maths through:

- Perspective and proportion in drawing
- Scale models and architectural design
- Geometry and spatial relationships
- Colour theory and ratios

By age 13, she was comfortable with mathematical concepts that many traditionally schooled peers found abstract --- because she'd always experienced maths as embedded in meaningful work.

Noah's Literacy Development (Systems Thinker)

Reading: By age 13, Noah was reading:

- Game design theory
- Programming documentation
- Fantasy novels with complex world-building
- Articles about systems and strategy

He read voraciously when topics interested him, but resisted arbitrary assigned reading. His parents trusted that engagement over compliance builds stronger readers.

Writing: Noah's writing developed through:

- Game design documents
- Devlogs explaining his thinking
- Tutorials teaching others his strategies
- Argumentative writing about game balance

His writing was logical, clear, and purposeful --- shaped by systems thinking.

Mathematics: Noah discovered he loved mathematics when he realised it was the language of systems:

- Probability in game design
- Optimisation and efficiency
- Logic and algorithms
- Statistical analysis of game mechanics

What had felt arbitrary in traditional school became fascinating when embedded in problems he cared about solving.

A Reassuring Truth

Every successful adult you know developed literacy and numeracy skills.

Most did it through traditional schooling --- but not because traditional methods are optimal. They succeeded despite the system's limitations, not because of its strengths.

Your child, learning through meaningful work with your attentive support, has every advantage those adults had --- plus:

- **Greater motivation** (purpose is built in)
- **Deeper understanding** (application is immediate)
- **More personalisation** (pace and format match the learner)
- **Stronger metacognition** (they understand how they learn)

Trust the process.

Watch for growth.

Adjust when needed.

The skills will come.

And when they do, they'll be anchored in meaning rather than memorisation --- which means they'll last.

Chapter 9: "But What About the Gaps?" --- Addressing the Fear of Missing Something

This chapter addresses the fear that keeps many parents awake at night:

What if we miss something essential?

It's the gap anxiety --- the worry that your child will reach adulthood missing a crucial piece of knowledge or skill because you didn't follow a prescribed curriculum.

Let me say this clearly:

Gaps are inevitable. They're also far less catastrophic than we've been led to believe.

The Myth of Complete Coverage

Traditional schooling operates on an assumption: if we expose students to everything important during their school years, they'll be prepared for life.

This assumption has three problems:

1. "Everything important" is impossible to define
Knowledge expands faster than any curriculum can accommodate. What's essential today may be irrelevant in a decade. The skills needed for emerging careers often don't exist in current curricula.

2. Exposure ≠ learning
Sitting through a unit on the water cycle doesn't mean you understand it. Most adults can't recall half of what they were "taught" in school. Exposure without engagement creates the illusion of learning, not the reality.

3. Gaps exist regardless of method
Every single adult has knowledge gaps --- including those who completed traditional schooling perfectly. Ask any adult about photosynthesis, the causes of World War I, or how to calculate percentages. Most will struggle despite "learning" these topics.

We all learn what we need when we need it.

The question isn't "How do we avoid gaps?"

The question is **"How do we equip our children to fill gaps independently when they encounter them?"**

The Real Skills That Matter

Decades of research on successful adults shows that what predicts thriving isn't how much content you covered in childhood.

It's whether you developed:

- **Curiosity**: The drive to keep learning
- **Resourcefulness**: The ability to find what you need
- **Persistence**: The willingness to struggle through difficulty
- **Confidence**: The belief that you can figure things out
- **Critical thinking**: The capacity to evaluate information
- **Communication**: The ability to share ideas clearly
- **Collaboration**: The skill of working with others

Learning Expeditions build exactly these capacities.

A child who has:

- Researched complex questions independently
- Struggled through problems and revised solutions
- Taught others what they've learnt
- Built things from scratch
- Collaborated on meaningful projects

… has developed far more durable capabilities than a child who memorised and forgot a standardised curriculum.

What Gaps Actually Look Like

Let's be honest about what "gaps" mean in practice.

Your child might:

- Not know all the bones in the human body
- Be unfamiliar with specific historical events (dates, battles, treaties)
- Not have memorised the periodic table
- Lack familiarity with certain literary classics
- Not know all the state capitals or countries on a map
- Have never studied ancient civilisations in detail

So what?

When they need to know anatomy, they'll learn it.
When history becomes relevant, they'll research it.
When chemistry matters, they'll study it.
When literature speaks to them, they'll read it.
When geography is needed, they'll explore it.

The gap isn't the problem. **The problem would be if they didn't know how to learn when gaps appear.**

Real Talk: My Own Gaps

As someone with traditional education through university, let me share my gaps:

- I can't remember most of the history I memorised
- I've forgotten virtually all trigonometry
- I read exactly three of the "classics" I was assigned (and hated two)
- My knowledge of science is embarrassingly patchy
- I couldn't label most countries on a blank map

These gaps haven't prevented me from:

- Having a successful career in education
- Writing this book
- Learning what I need when I need it
- Being a thoughtful, engaged citizen

Your child's gaps won't define them either.

The "Just-in-Time" Model vs. "Just-in-Case" Model

Traditional education is **just-in-case learning**:

"You might need to know this someday, so learn it now."

The problem? Most of it gets forgotten before "someday" arrives. The brain doesn't retain information it can't connect to meaning or use.

Expedition-based learning is **just-in-time learning**:

"You need to know this now to do what matters to you."

This approach creates:

- **Stronger retention** (because learning is purposeful)
- **Deeper understanding** (because application is immediate)
- **Greater motivation** (because relevance is obvious)
- **Better transfer** (skills connect to real contexts)

Adults learn this way naturally. We don't study Spanish "just in case" we visit Spain someday --- we study it when we book the trip. We don't learn spreadsheet formulas abstractly --- we learn them when we need to organise our budget.

Why shouldn't children learn the same way?

The Gaps That Do Matter

I'm not arguing that all gaps are harmless.

Some foundational capabilities do need attention:

Core Literacies (covered in Chapter 8):

- Reading fluency and comprehension
- Written communication
- Mathematical reasoning
- Critical evaluation of information

Life Skills:

- Basic cooking and nutrition
- Financial literacy (budgeting, saving, understanding money and debt)
- Safety awareness (physical, digital, social)
- Social and emotional regulation
- Basic household management

Civic Literacy:

- How government and democracy work
- Understanding rights and responsibilities
- Evaluating information sources
- Participating in community

Relational Skills:

- Communication and conflict resolution
- Empathy and perspective-taking
- Collaboration and compromise
- Boundaries and consent

These aren't subjects to "cover" in units --- they're capacities to develop over time, often through expeditions and daily life.

Notice what's not on this list: memorised facts, comprehensive content coverage, or knowledge tested once and forgotten.

How to Address Gaps When They Appear

The beauty of homeschooling is responsiveness.

When you notice a gap that matters:

1. Assess Whether It's Urgent

Does your child need this now? Or is it something they'll naturally encounter later?

A twelve-year-old who doesn't know about World War II isn't behind --- they'll encounter it when it's relevant.

A sixteen-year-old who wants to study medicine but struggles with basic biology does need targeted intervention.

Urgency depends on current goals and near-term needs, not arbitrary grade-level standards.

2. Address It Directly

When a gap matters, address it without shame or panic:

"You're interested in economics but don't understand percentages yet. Let's spend a week on that."

"You want to read this philosophy but need stronger comprehension strategies first. Let's work on that."

Direct instruction has its place. Use it strategically.

3. Connect It to Existing Interests

"This historical period connects to the story you're writing. Want to research it?"

"Understanding chemistry would help you understand cooking better. Interested?"

Gaps close faster when connected to meaning.

4. Trust Their Readiness

Sometimes a topic doesn't stick because the child isn't developmentally ready. Their brain needs more maturity or prior knowledge.

That's not failure --- it's development.

Return to it in six months or a year. You'll often be amazed at how quickly they grasp what previously felt impossible.

Most gaps close themselves when learning is personalised and purposeful.

The "Catch-Up" Myth

Parents worry: *"If we don't cover everything now, my child will have to 'catch up' later."*

This assumes learning is a race with a fixed destination.

It's not.

Your child isn't behind peers --- they're on a different path. Skills developed through deep, meaningful work often surpass surface-level knowledge acquired through coverage.

And here's the secret: **adolescents and adults learn faster than children.**

A motivated sixteen-year-old can learn a year's worth of traditional curriculum in weeks when they decide it matters. An eighteen-year-old preparing for university can master chemistry or algebra more quickly than a twelve-year-old forced through it prematurely.

Cognitive development matters. Sometimes waiting is the fastest path.

Trust that.

What About University Requirements?

This concern deserves its own attention, which may be a topic in a future book in the series.

The short version:

Universities care about:

- Demonstrated capability and intellectual curiosity
- Independence and initiative
- Clear communication and critical thinking
- Evidence of deep learning in any domain
- Unique perspectives and experiences

They care far less than you think about whether you memorised every item on a standard curriculum.

In fact, homeschoolers who've pursued deep, self-directed learning often have **stronger university applications** than their traditionally schooled peers --- precisely because of their unusual depth.

Those gaps represent focus, passion, and mastery.

Admissions officers recognise that.

A Practical Strategy: The "Core + Flex" Model

If gap anxiety is keeping you paralysed, try this framework:

Core (20-30% of time):

- Reading, writing, maths fundamentals
- Skills needed for current expeditions
- Gaps you've identified as genuinely important now
- Legal requirements for your jurisdiction

Flex (70-80% of time):

- Learning Expeditions
- Child-directed exploration
- Deep dives into interests
- Unstructured time for play, rest, and emergence

This creates security (you're ensuring foundations) whilst maintaining the freedom that makes homeschooling powerful.

You're not abandoning rigour --- you're redefining it.

The "Spiral Curriculum" of Real Life

Here's something traditional schooling gets wrong:

It assumes topics must be taught in sequence, once, at the "right" age.

But real learning spirals. You encounter concepts multiple times, at different levels, throughout life:

- A child learns about weather through observation and play
- Later, they study meteorology during a climate expedition
- As a teen, they understand weather systems through physics
- As an adult, they follow weather news with sophisticated understanding

Each encounter builds on the last. Nothing is "missed" forever --- it's simply encountered when meaningful.

Trust the spiral.

Assessing Readiness for Independence

The ultimate measure of homeschool success isn't whether your child knows everything.

It's whether they've become an independent learner who:

- **Identifies what they need to know**: "I need to understand this to do what I want"
- **Finds resources and information**: Libraries, internet, experts, experimentation
- **Persists through difficulty**: "This is hard, but I can figure it out"
- **Evaluates their own understanding**: "Do I actually get this, or did I just memorise it?"
- **Seeks help when stuck**: Asking good questions, finding mentors
- **Transfers learning across contexts**: "This is similar to something I already know"

If these capacities are developing, gaps are just opportunities for future learning.

Your child has become a lifelong learner --- which is the entire point.

Questions to Ask Instead of "Are There Gaps?"

Shift from gap-anxiety to capability-confidence:

✗ "Does my child know everything a traditionally schooled child knows?"

■ "Can my child learn what they need when they need it?"

- "Are we covering all the subjects?"

- "Is my child developing deep capability in meaningful areas?"

- "Will this gap hurt them later?"

- "Is this gap actually preventing anything important right now?"

- "Should I panic?"

- "What evidence of growth do I actually see?"

The reframe is powerful.

A Reassuring Perspective

Some of history's most accomplished people had enormous gaps:

- Einstein struggled with languages and many areas of mathematics
- Darwin never mastered mathematics beyond basic arithmetic
- Many successful authors never studied literature formally
- Countless innovators dropped out or rejected traditional paths

What made them successful wasn't comprehensive coverage.

It was deep engagement in what mattered to them plus the confidence to learn anything else they needed.

That's exactly what you're building in your child.

- **Note for Diverse Learners:**
  For twice-exceptional learners --- children who are gifted in some areas but struggle in others --- gaps are normal and expected. The goal isn't to force weak areas to match strong ones. It's to build on strengths whilst providing support for challenges. These learners often become remarkable adults precisely because their education honoured their uneven development. Their "gaps" become irrelevant because their strengths are extraordinary.

Final Thought

Every expert in every field has enormous gaps in their knowledge.

What makes them experts isn't comprehensive coverage --- it's deep capability in their domain plus the confidence to learn anything else they need.

That's exactly what you're building in your child.

The gaps aren't failures.

They're proof that you prioritised depth over breadth, meaning over memorisation, and capability over coverage.

Trust that.

What's Next?

If this book resonated with you:

> 📥 **Download your free templates:** https://dennispack.gumroad.com/l/theintegratedhomeschool

> ⭐ **Leave a review:** Your honest feedback helps other families discover this approach

> 📖 **Watch for Book 2:** If you download the Tools & Templates, you will receive an email when it is available.

> 💬 **Connect with others:** Search your favorite social media platforms for homeschool groups focused on inquiry-based or project-based learning.

Remember you can download your free Tools & Templates from the following link:

https://dennispack.gumroad.com/l/theintegratedhomeschool

Access is optional and not required to use this book.

About the Author

D.R. Pack is an educator with over 30 years of experience in classroom teaching, curriculum development, and educational technology across five countries. His career has encompassed roles as a science teacher, outdoor education coordinator, curriculum developer, Director of Studies, and educational technology consultant --- taking him from Oregon classrooms to remote Pacific Island communities in Kiribati, Fiji, and the Solomon Islands.

Pack's teaching philosophy centers on learner-centered, inquiry-based education that honors each student's unique strengths and connects learning to real-world contexts. Whether coordinating outdoor education programs and teaching biology in South Australia, or developing tablet-based learning resources in the Pacific, he witnessed the same pattern: depth of engagement matters more than breadth of coverage.

His international work in under-resourced educational environments shaped a crucial conviction: the best learning doesn't happen when you try to replicate what schools do. It happens when you design around how individual learners actually think. Meaningful learning doesn't require expensive curriculum --- it requires thoughtful design, genuine curiosity, and respect for how children learn.

This book grew from years of staffroom conversations with fellow educators who loved the work of Sir Ken Robinson and Eddie Woo, and who had all seen the benefits of student-centered, hands-on learning. But they were frustrated by the difficulty of implementing such approaches within traditional school constraints. When Dennis integrated these philosophies together, it became obvious that the best place to implement such a system would be in a homeschool environment --- though the framework benefits all teachers, whether at home or not.

The Integrated Homeschool draws on educational models from Sir Ken Robinson, Eddie Woo, and Expeditionary Learning schools, adapted for the unique freedoms and challenges of homeschooling. It represents Pack's conviction that meaningful education is possible anywhere --- you just need to know what actually matters.